101 U
Sever

Theresa George

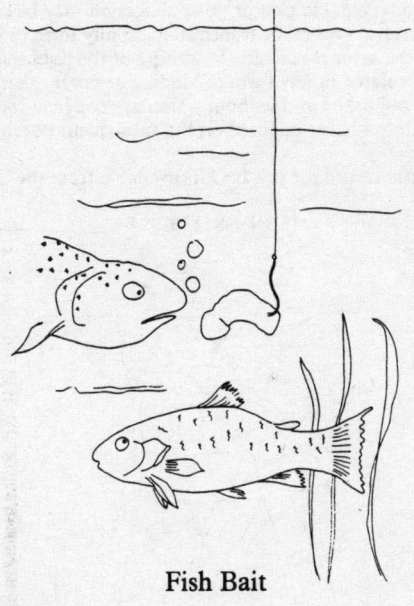

Fish Bait

Michael O'Mara Books Limited

To all the men in my life who cringe and cross their legs whenever
I mention this book

First published in 1994 by
Michael O'Mara Books Limited
9 Lion Yard
Tremadoc Road
London SW4 7NQ

Copyright © 1994 Theresa George

Printed and bound in England by Cox and Wyman, Reading.

A CIP catalogue record for this book is available from the British Library

ISBN 1-85479-994-0

Opera Glasses

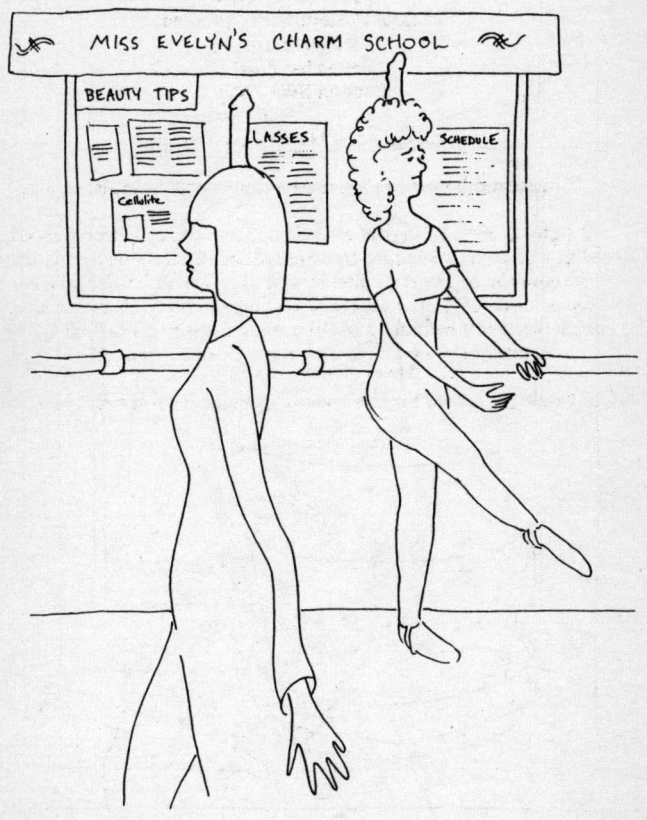

Deportment Device

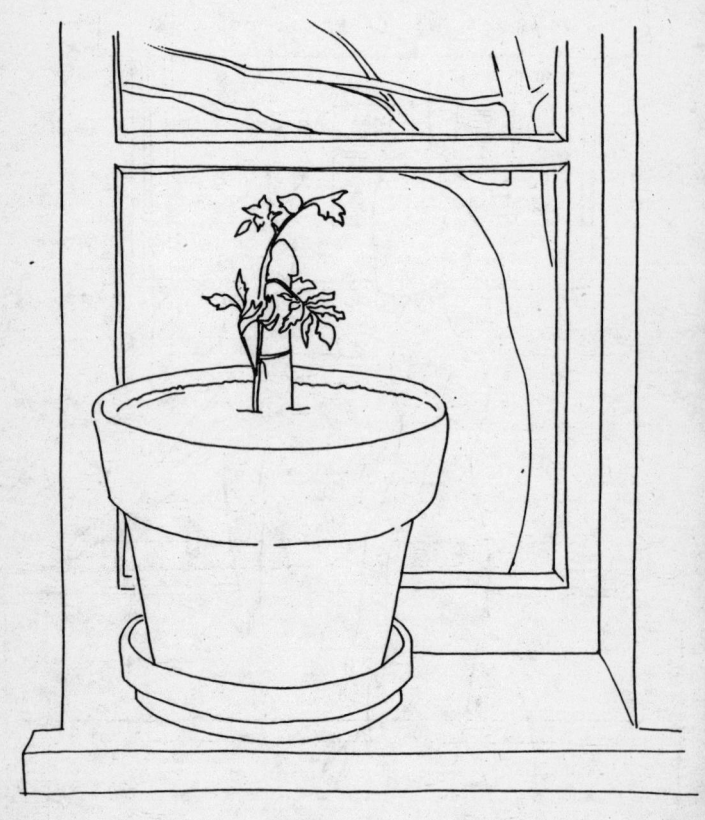

Seedling-Support Stake

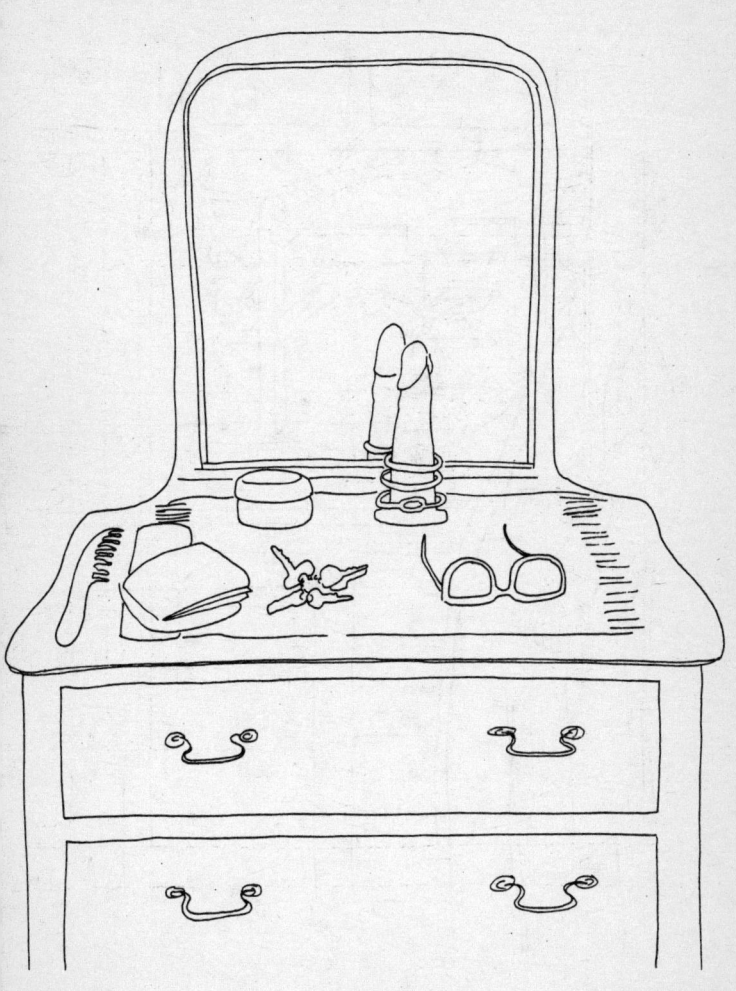

Ring Tree

Mug Tree

Salt and Pepper Shakers

Frying-Pan Handle

Mortar and Pestle

Corn-on-the-Cob Holders

Cocktail-Swizzle Sticks

Cake Decorator

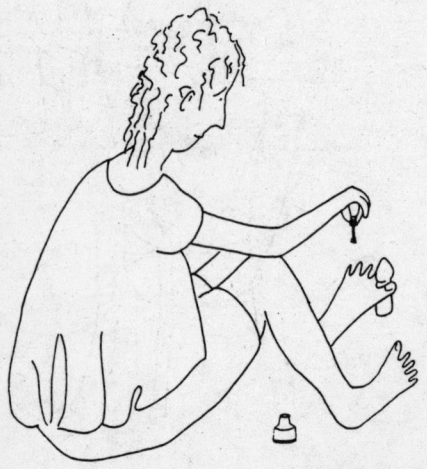

Finger and Toe Separator

Bud Vase

Unique Pendant

Skipping-Rope Handles

Seed-Hole Digger

Rolling Pin

Wine Cork

Turkey Baster

Garden-Hose Power Nozzle

Doughnut-Hole Maker

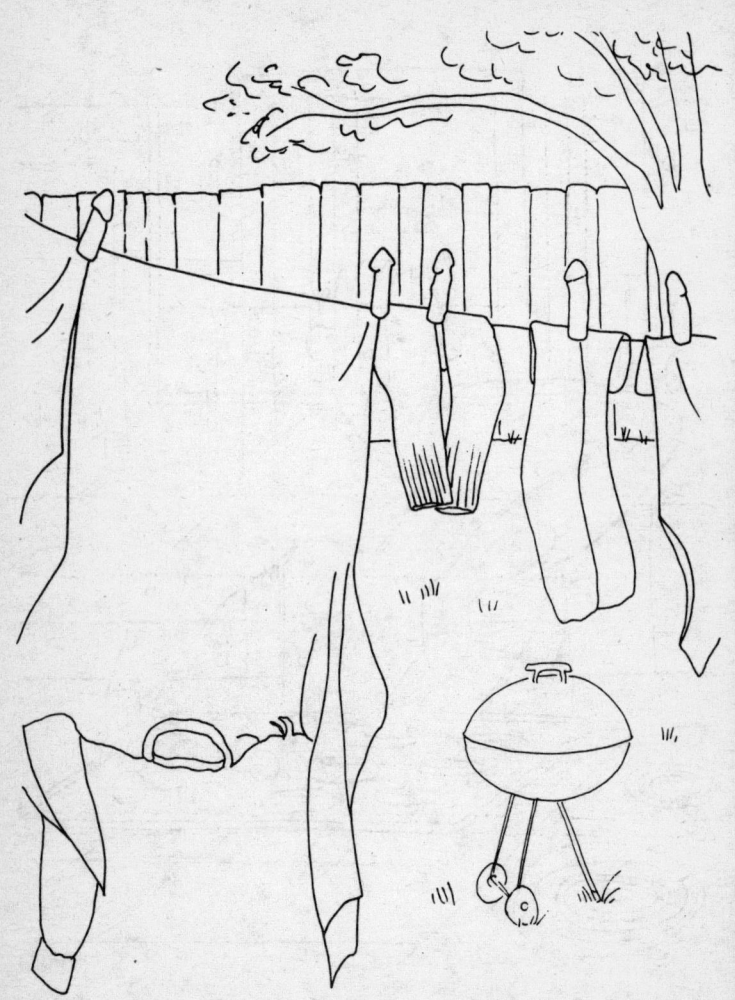

Clothes Pegs

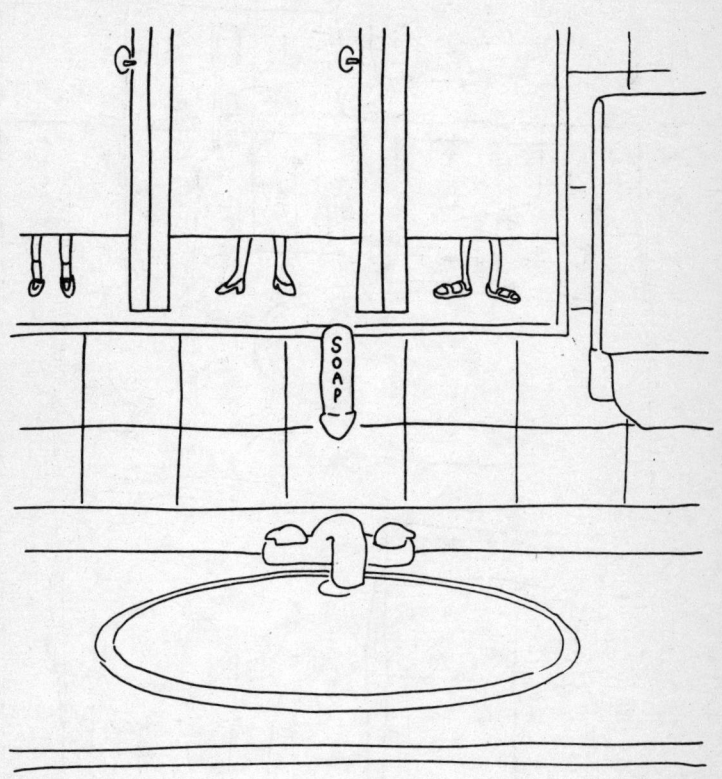

Soap Dispenser

Toothbrush Holder

Umbrella Handle

Toilet-Bowl Scrubber

Bird Perch

Phone Dialler

Candle Holder

Gear Shift

Executive-Briefcase Handle

Key Ring

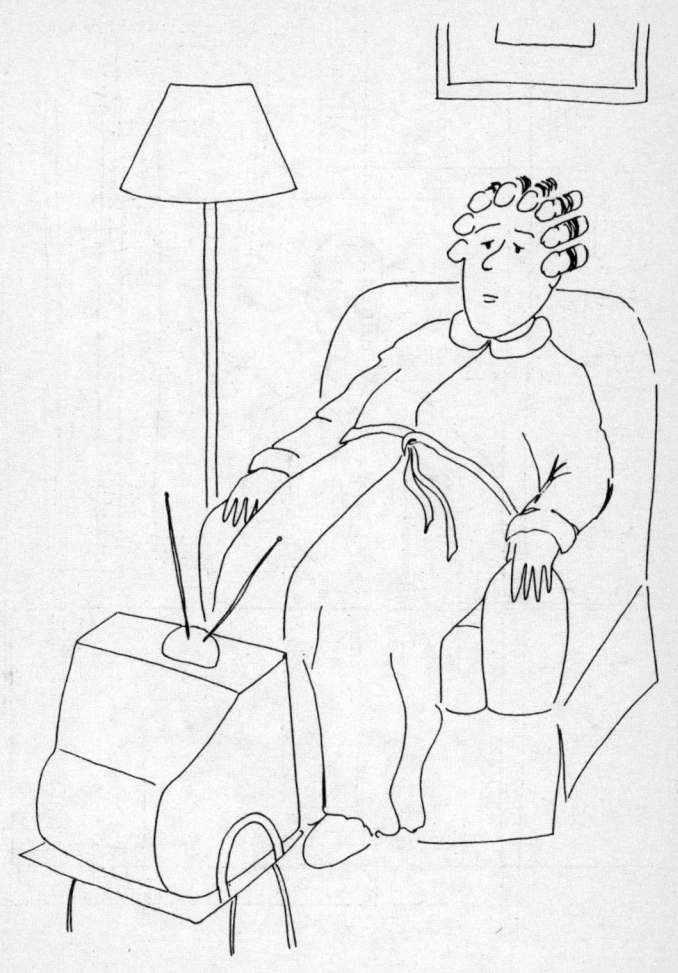

Hair Rollers

Self-Inking Stamp

Book Ends

Finger Puppets

Water Pistols

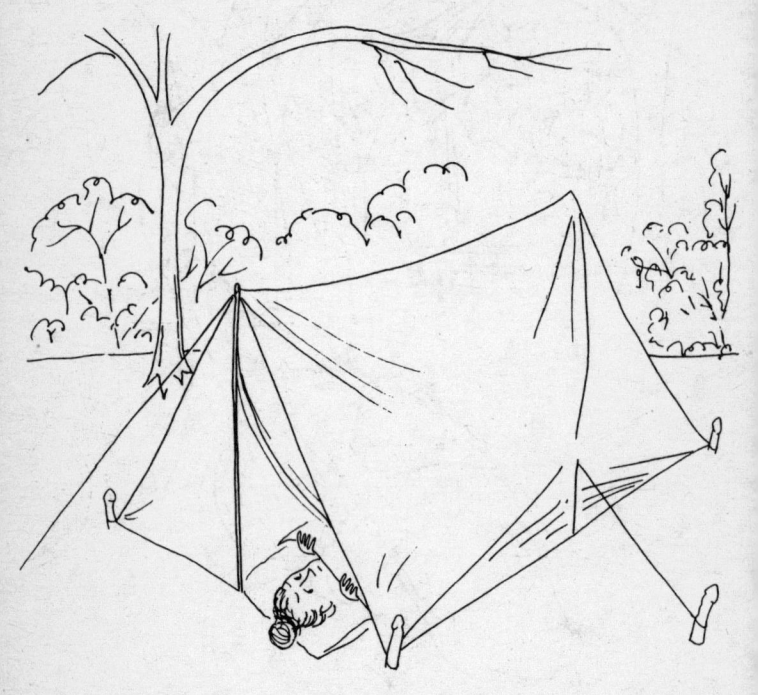

Tent Stakes

Bicycle Handles

Aquarium Accessory

Bowling Pins

Bird Call

Drum Sticks

Conducting Baton

Artist's Paintbrush

Billiard Cues

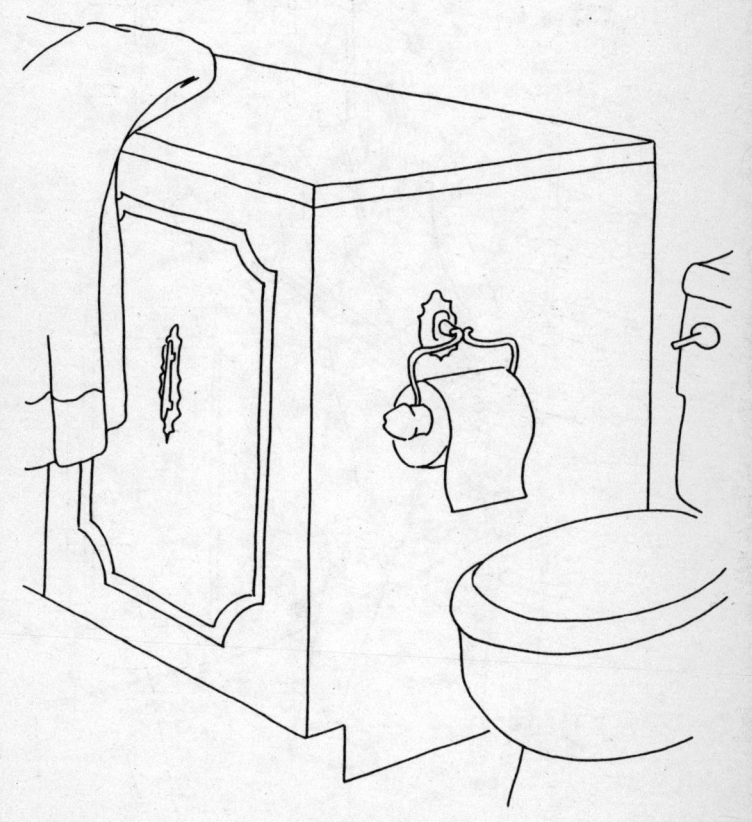

Loo-Roll Holder

Guitar Pick

Violin Bow

Piano Pedals

Hat and Coat Hooks

Dog-Fetching Toy

Dog Chew

Name-Card Holder

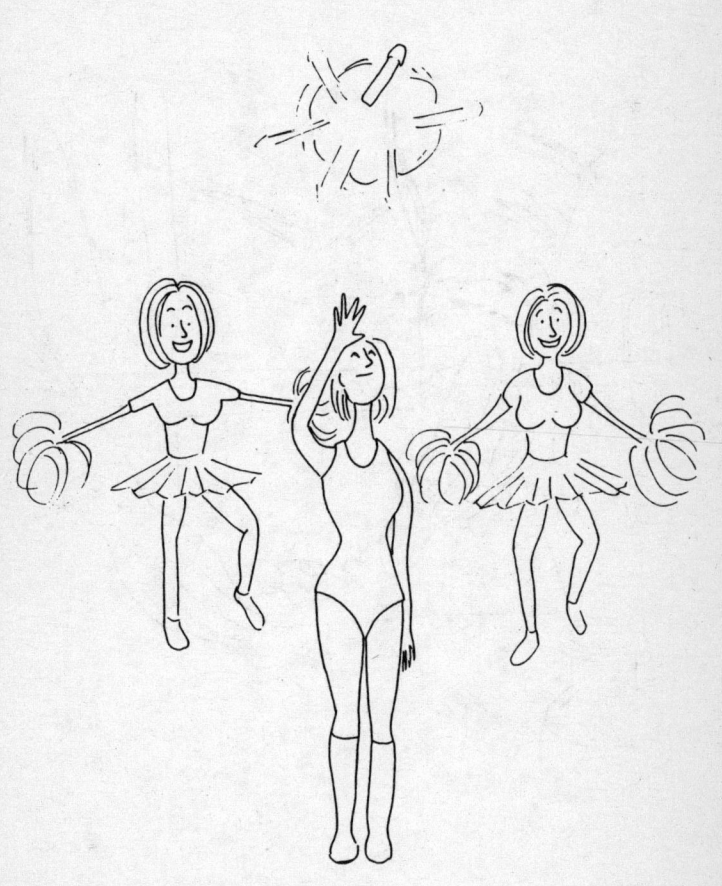

Cheerleading Baton

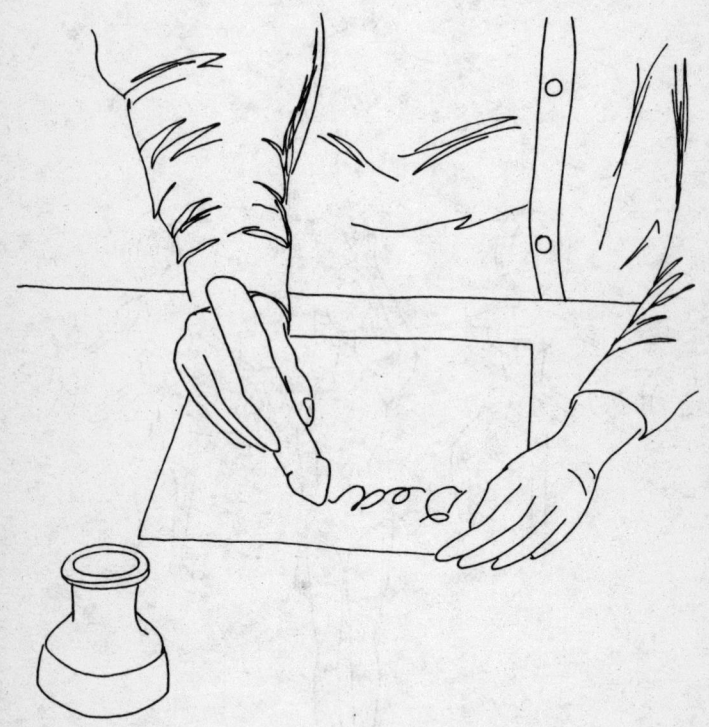

Ink Pen

Pendulum

Hockey Puck

Drawer Handles

Kite-String Handle

Relay-Race Baton

Television Antennae

Vacuum Hose

Hot-Willie Party Game

Pick-Up Sticks Game

Drawing Straws

Hop-Scotch Marker

Reading the Runes

Shower Head

Page Turner

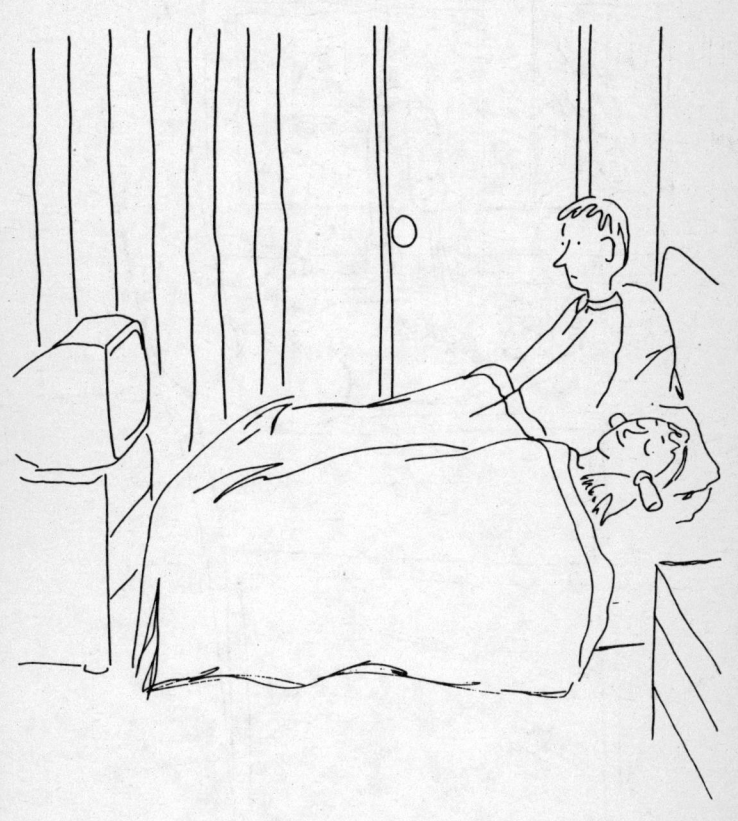

Ear Plugs

Faucet Nozzle

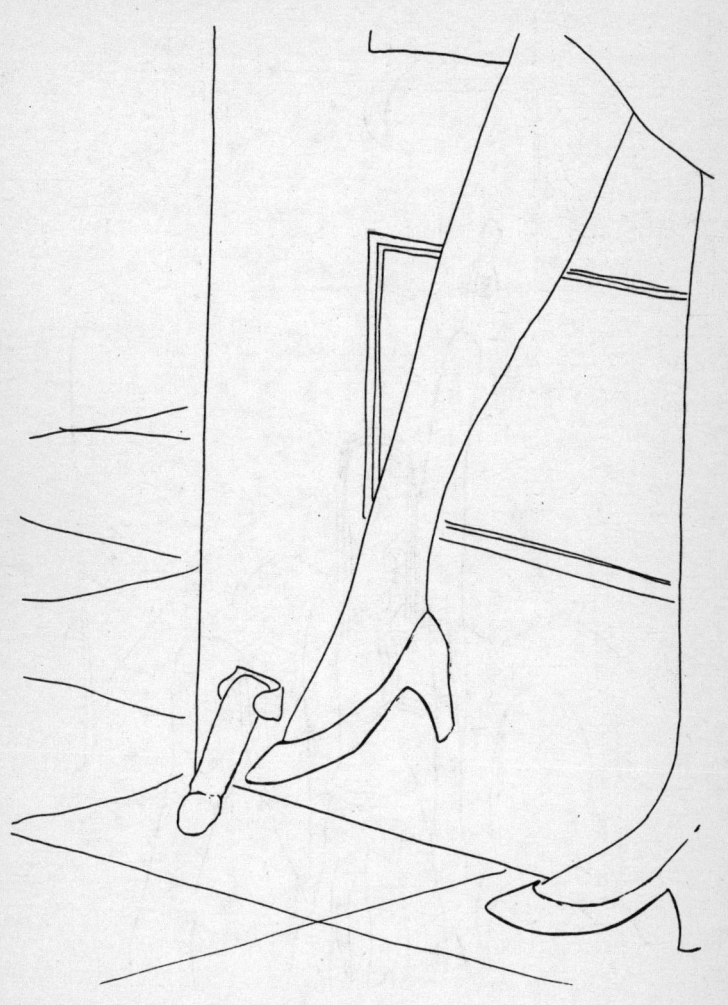

Door Stop

New-Age Witch Wand

Decorative Clock Hands

Windscreen Wipers

Personal-Reminder Willie

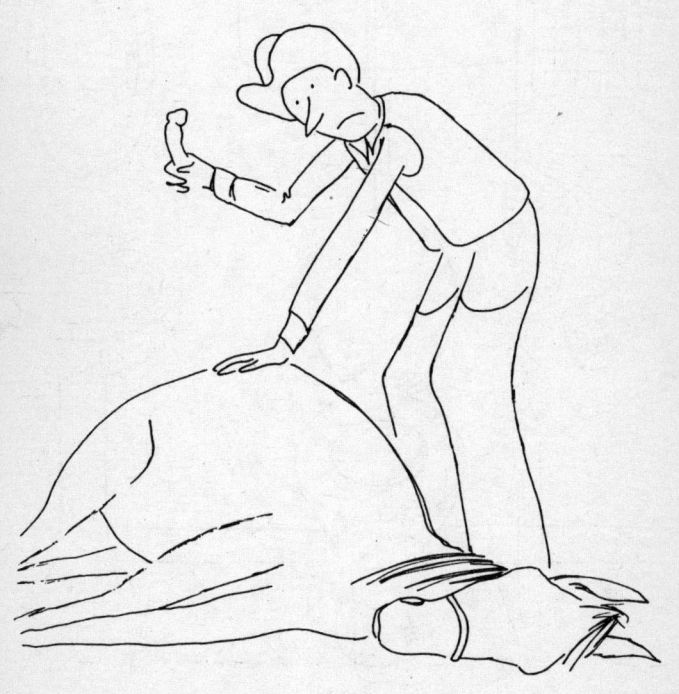

Flogging a Dead Horse

Toilet Flush

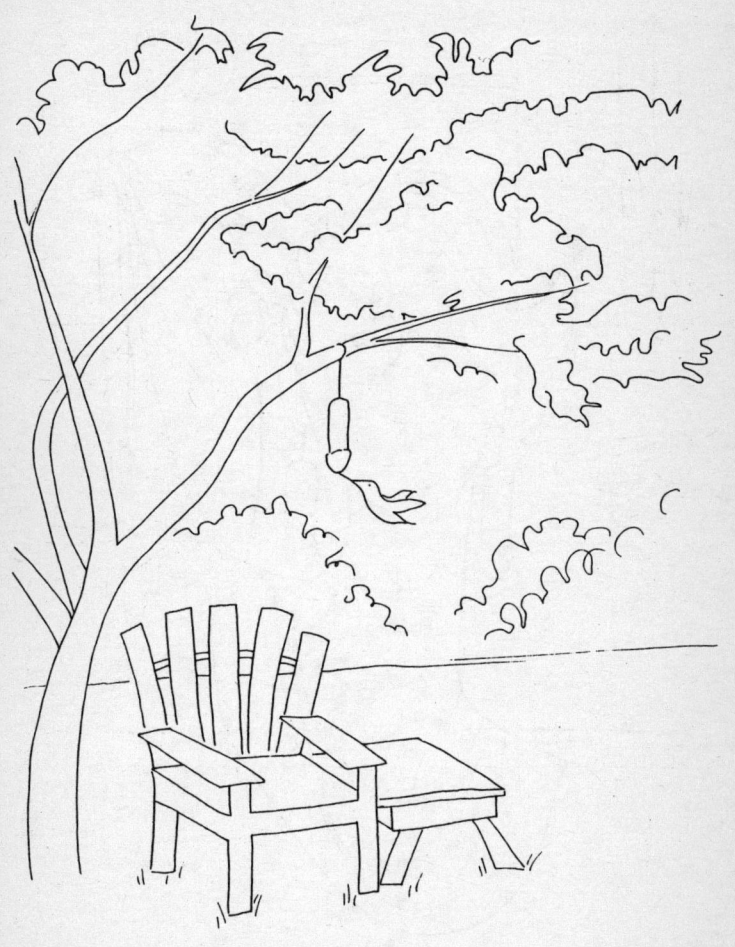

Bird Feeder

Earrings

Plumb Line

Police Baton

Make-up Applicator

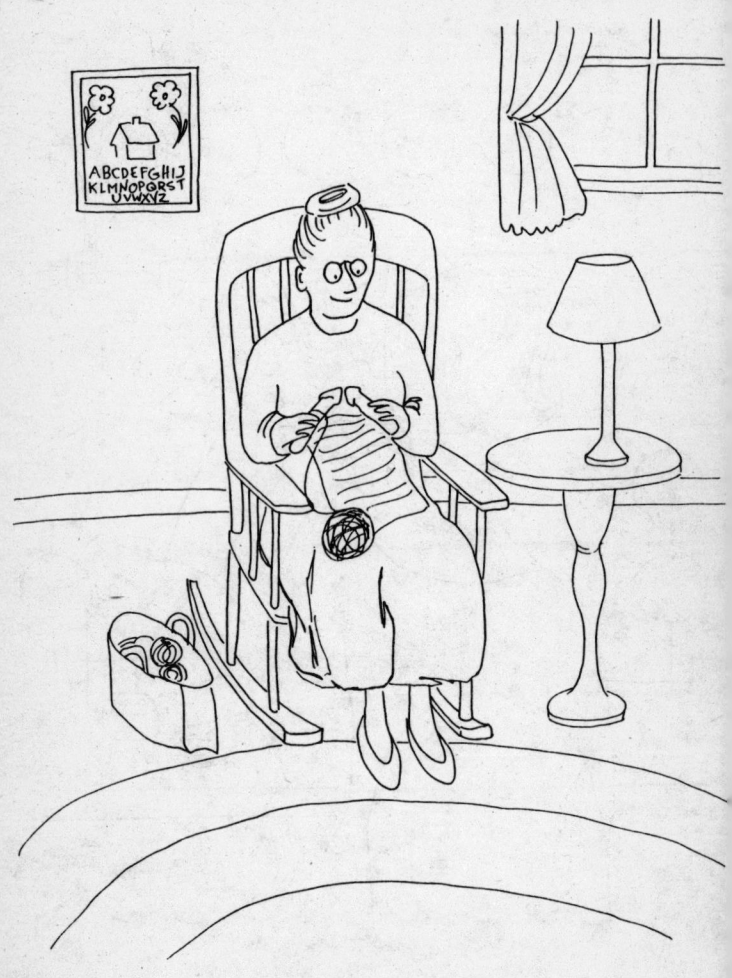

Knitting Needles

Riding Crop

Telephone Receiver

Garden Ornaments

Darts

Pointer

Trumpet Mute

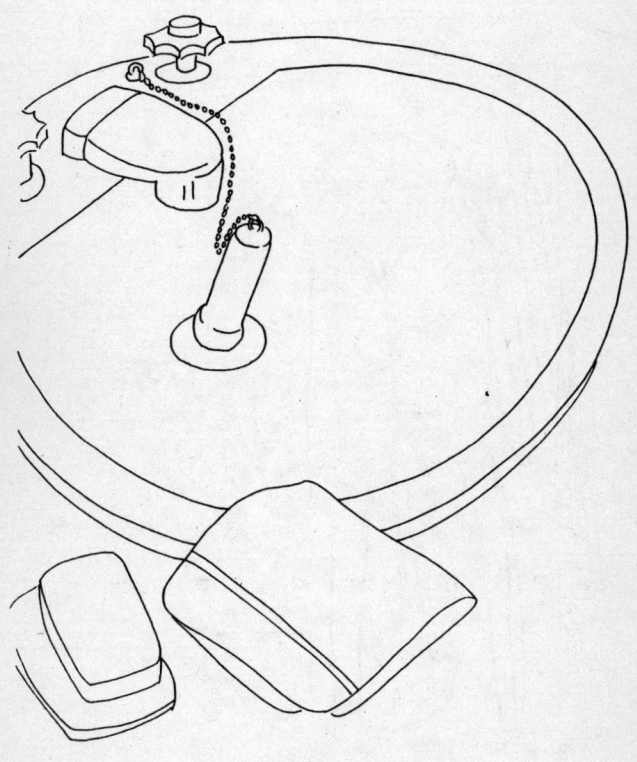

Sink Plug

Flagellation Tool

Garden Markers

Ring-Toss Game

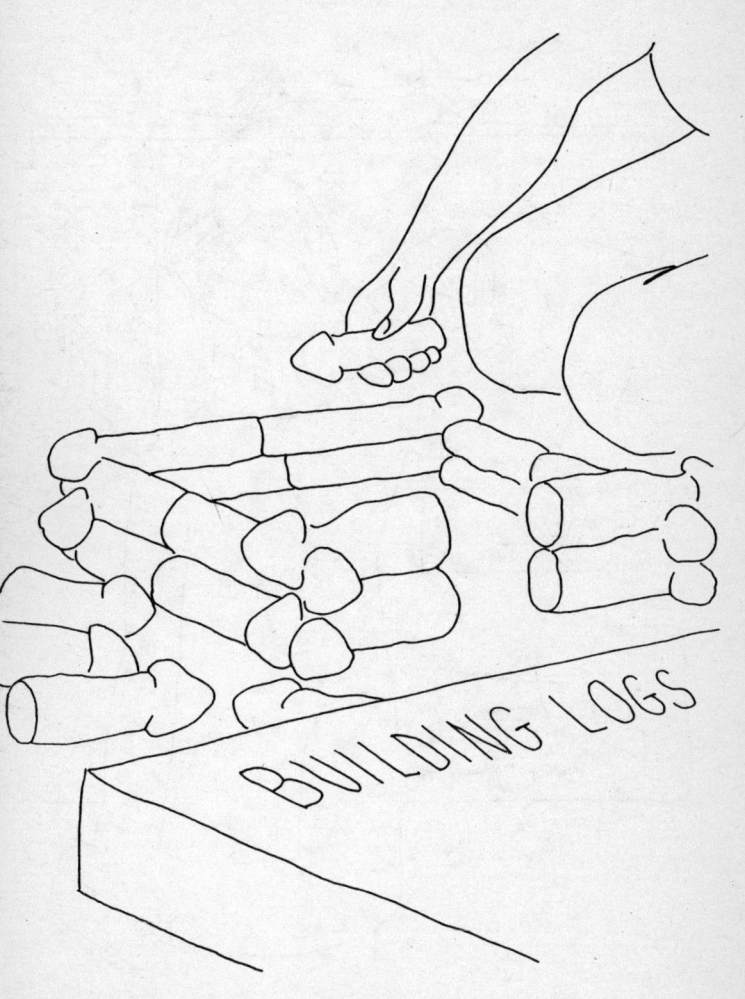

BUILDING LOGS

Erector Set

Hat Decoration